SOCIAL ENGINEERING

Investigative and *Deceptive* *Methods Used* in *Corporate* and *Private Settings*

Christopher B. Fields

Copyright © 2024 Christopher B. Fields

All rights reserved.

ISBN: 9798305079142

> "If you leave a door unlocked, it's only a matter of time before a stranger walks in."

-C.B. FIELDS

CONTENTS

1. WHAT IS SOCIAL ENGINEERING?
2. HUMAN INTELLIGENCE
3. OPEN-SOURCE INTELLIGENCE
4. UNDERSTANDING COMMUNICATION
5. SIX TYPES OF COMMON SOCIAL ENGINEERING ATTACKS
6. GENERAL SECURITY MEASURES
7. SOCIAL ENGINEERING IN THE MEDIA
8. HOW DO YOU PREVENT SOCIAL ENGINEERING?
9. RED FLAGS
10. THE MOST IMPORTANT ELEMENT

SOCIAL ENGINEERING:

Investigative and Deceptive Methods Used in Corporate and Private Settings

I often like to compare language experts with turtles. You see, turtles have two additional legs that are contained within their body, and underneath the outside of the shell. Scientists believe that due to evolution, these extremities have developed in an event that a turtle loses an outer leg from an attack within their environment.

Language experts are quite similar. The unknowns

within each conversation will sometimes cause the language expert to pivot, therefore evolve to the conversation in hopes of keeping a healthy line of communication.

However, the problem with this is that turtles, in fact, do not have two additional legs. It was a very simple lie, but unfortunately, between 50 and 60 percent of people that read that statement will immediately believe it.

Why is that? Is it because you're completely oblivious to the biology of turtles?

Maybe it's because you assume the author of this book is a "figure of authority"?

Maybe it's because your attention was diverted from the statement and more toward to the comparison of language experts and turtles.

Maybe it's because you simply do not care.

The point here is that the majority of language never reaches the conscious level of the listener. Listeners make their conscious decisions from the building blocks of their subconscious mind, and the subconscious mind retains all of the surrounding information.

Language professionals, social engineers, and hackers have learned how to use this method to exploit conversations for personal gain.

Every single hack, no matter the type, begins with the human, first. It's logical if you think about it. Why spend years of training trying to understand the specifics behind Cybersecurity when you can simply extract detailed information from a person's mouth? This is nothing new, however, attacks by the use of social engineering have become more common throughout the technological age. With that being said, if the top government intelligence agency in the world can be hacked, rest assured, you are far away from being "safe". Now, you must understand what steps you can take to prevent breaches for yourself and your organization, and to simplify that, you must "think" like the social engineer to "combat" the social engineer.

LEGAL DISCLAIMER:

Before you proceed in learning about the practice of Social Engineering, it's imperative to understand that this information is provided for "educational purposes only". In order to realize potential security vulnerabilities you are presented with each day, you must understand how Social Engineers obtain and use your information from their point-of-view.

WHAT IS SOCIAL ENGINEERING?

Social Engineering is the exercise of obtaining detailed information of personnel in private and corporate settings by the use of Open-Source Intelligence, Human Intelligence, and psychological methods. This information is then used to exploit and compromise the credentials of organizations and individuals, primarily for financial gain to the attacker. When people hear the phrase, "Social Engineering" or "Attack", they typically assume it's in reference to Cybersecurity hacks. This is only partially true. Social engineering is a stand-alone technique that doesn't require the use of computers whatsoever. However, almost 90% of cyber-attacks rely on social engineering to be successful.

WHY IS SOCIAL ENGINEERING USED?

Social engineering tactics are fine-tuned, persuasive conversational tactics used to extract personal information from individuals and companies.

The groups of people that use this form of tactic includes; Detectives, on-site thieves, hackers, salespeople, and yes, even potential dating partners.

In most cases, this is simply performed to gain access to a person's funds in a variety of ways. It's quite surprising how many people will simply hand over their personal-identifiable information to a complete stranger or random message they received. In an age where almost every social media site or account is linked to a third-party app that uses your banking account, the severity of each hack rises each year.

Aside from a hacker potentially having access to your

banking information, they may also access your close friends and their contact information. This is like "pulling a thread" for a hacker. In many cases, a stranger can access one of your contacts on behalf of you to gain some of their personal information. It's a bit easier acting as someone close, wouldn't you agree?

Companies have a similar issue with losing access to their entire clientele information being leaked. Sometimes, this can be detrimental to the trust of a company.

However, there are ethical work practices that attempt to gain information from competitor companies. Competitive Intelligence is the practice of legally researching an entire company, under the scope of law, to provide feedback for a competing company. Corporate Espionage is, of course, illegal in the United States, but this type of research is conducted professionally.

With that being said, during Competitive Intelligence Investigations, a company under review may receive multiple phone and email communications to learn more about their company. This could include things like pricing, clients, decision-makers, etc. What may seem harmless to an employee can be harmful from a larger perspective.

SOCIAL ENGINEERING STATISTICS

I feel like it's safe to say that every person with a phone or internet access will eventually encounter a potential Social Engineering hack within their lifetime. It's an unfortunate part of the modern world. Therefore, we can assume that 100% of people are at risk on a daily-basis.

Considering social engineering attacks conducted on businesses, due to better reporting systems, we can have a better view on the amount of successful and unsuccessful attacks that are reported each year.

In fact, social engineering attacks tend to be the #1 threat to all businesses. These types of attacks cost businesses between three to six trillion dollars each year, with the average cost of each attack being approximately $130,000.

While attackers know there are deep financial pockets within company bank accounts, they seek out weak employee links to fulfill their gain. Therefore, it's no surprise that over 60% of businesses are confronted with social engineering attacks each year.

With false emails being the easiest route of scamming an organization, it's important to know that on average, 45% of employees open suspicious emails, with 60% of those employees being new-hires.

HOW DO INDIVIDUALS OBTAIN INFORMATION ABOUT YOU?

Obtaining information about an individual or organization is comprised by three parts; Human Intelligence (HUMINT), Open-Source Intelligence (OSINT), and Social Engineering.

These three forms of information-extraction tend to

overlap each other, and each serve a crucial part to understanding another person.

Over the next few chapters, we will go through the meaning of each part, and step-by-step methods to use this information from a social engineer's point-of-view.

HUMAN INTELLIGENCE (HUMINT)

HUMINT stands for Human Intelligence. Human Intelligence is the process of obtaining information from a person or group by the means of person-to-person observation and surveillance.

Whether a person is aware of it or not, they carry around identifiable information on a daily basis. This information is on display for the world to see. Though some things we can't help but to display in public view, there are others that are simply not necessary. As I mentioned before, small bits of useless information can turn into an array of details for someone attempting to hack you by "pulling the thread".

Let's go over some common ways of obtaining Human Intelligence, and which type of information can be conveyed from each piece;

VEHICLE STICKERS

People love to display their pride right on the back of their vehicle, and rightfully so. The problem with that is that each sticker you slap on the back reduces your privacy, and sometimes, by a lot.

Which school does your child go to? What is the name of your workplace? Are you a "wife of a police officer"? Is your child in the U.S. Military?

Does your license plate have your name on it? A specialized plate?

Does your back windshield show your initials written

in cute, catchy letters?

The list goes on, and on, and on. Some will think, "what could you possibly do with that type of information"? A lot, actually. It really depends if you ever come under the radar of another person, stalker, hacker, or maybe just someone you really aggravated in traffic.

In addition, the type of people seeking your information will take these notes to add at a later date.

You see, maybe a person only has bits and pieces of information about you. Maybe they can't determine your exact vehicle or which house you live in on your street. However, with someone that gives additional clues from the back of their vehicle, an investigator or ill-willed person can quickly conclude your identity by a process of elimination.

LEFT HAND OR RIGHT HAND

Reading this title, you may find something like being left or right-handed to be completely insignificant. In many cases, it is. However, there are still a few, very good points we can utilize from this.

Giving information to the public whether you're right or left-handed is fairly easy. Which hand is dominate? Which hand do you write with? Which hand do you use to pick up objects? Yes, there are individuals out there that use both. I am actually one of them. Nevertheless, that's a rare percentage of the population and nothing is ever 100%.

Nothing.

For starters, let's assume you're a left-handed person. The amount of left-handed people are far less than those who use their right hand. This is a quick rapport-builder to a social engineer that recognizes that fact. Even if a social engineer is right-handed, they can simply use a question like, "this world really isn't designed for the left-handers, is it?

This may be followed up with, "Oh you're left-handed, too"?

Quick rapport by easily determining which dominate hand the listener is using. You now have a shoe in the door.

In other scenarios where you suspect someone may be carrying a firearm in their pants or jacket, after quickly determining their dominate hand, the assumption of which side the firearm is hidden and will be drawn from increases. The difference in that half-to-one second can be the difference between life or death for law enforcement, investigators, security personnel, or just the average person sitting in a coffee shop.

FAMILY PHOTOS

Family photos are very common on social media sites and office desks. Naturally, people feel motivated by showing off their loved ones. There is nothing wrong with this. However, as I mentioned earlier, for each piece of information you give out, you sacrifice a bit of security in exchange.

Let's assume you post a public or profile photo of your daughter onto social media with the title, "Natalie's Kindergarten Graduation". It's common. It's simple. It's nice.

A social engineer or hacker can look at the same photo, take notes of the information given, and attempt a social engineering attack.

For instance; Your photo gives the name of your daughter and presumably the school, in which, your daughter is graduating.

From this point, what is stopping a hacker from calling you with this information? Let's say the social engineer pretends to be an administrative employee with Natalie's new or former school, and advises you that there is an issue transferring her information?

Now, they need specific information from you to "correct the records". Date of birth, social security number, current address, bus route, etc. The list is endless.

I definitely wouldn't say that anyone should get paranoid about their family photos on social media, but it's important to understand how tiny bits of information can be pulled from some of the most harmless items.

Hopefully by the end of this book, you will view photos in a different light.

SIGN-IN SHEETS

Have you ever walked into a facility and had to fill out a sign-in sheet? Name, contact number, time, reason you are here, etc.?

I have always found this practice a bit unprofessional, especially when that facility is a hospital or doctor's office.

If you think about it, what is stopping a stranger from walking in, viewing the sign-in sheet, and walking out with details about each patient?

Nothing.

With that information, a social engineer can call anyone from the list, ask for someone by name, list their issue and which time they were there. The patient, of course, would assume it's the health facility calling because who else would have that information? From there, the hacker can ask for more details like a credit card number, social security number, date of birth, emergency contact, etc.

If using a sign-in sheet is a must, make sure you're as vague as possible with the information you give. If the information you give doesn't suffice, a receptionist can always ask you at a later date.

RECEIPTS

As I have explained, Human Intelligence and Open-Source Intelligence often overlap. The use of obtaining information from a receipt would be a very good example of that. In addition, the use of receipts can show you how the "pulling the thread" method is performed.

If you have ever been given a bill from a restaurant, nine out of ten times the name of the server is listed at the top of your bill. This is done to track the orders and tips of each server. Therefore, when the server arrives to work, they log in to their account. Each order is tracked, and when you receive the bill, the name of the server is provided at the top. As insignificant as this may seem, there are many people out there that are willing to use this information as a starting point.

Let's hypothetically say for whatever purpose that an individual is attempting to learn everything possible about a random restaurant server they have encountered.

After discovering the server's name from the bill, they now have a starting point. Can this individual simply ask the server's name? Yes, however, the individual would need to break the rhythm of a typical server-to-customer relationship. This could potentially set off a "red flag".

After obtaining the name, we can now add that to the name of the establishment. Has this person interacted with the social media page of this restaurant? Maybe yes, maybe no. If not, there's a very good chance that they're friends with another server or owner that has.

From that point, the individual would screen social media pages of the owner and other servers, looking for the name listed on their bill.

Almost always is this an efficient way of finding a person on social media. Once that page is found, an entire door opens for the "individual".

TATTOOS

Tattoos are a great way of showing the world the things you take pride in the most. Some people would say that their tattoos are simply random and have no meaning. I would disagree. There's clues behind each tattoo, even if they seem random. A random tattoo can tell you a lot about their interests or personality traits.

As for tattoos that are more personal, that one is a given.

Has this person served in the military? What are the initials of their child/children? Did their best friend or family pass away? When? Are they a musician? Are they religious? The list goes on, and on, and on.

When you're "pulling the thread", these clues begin to add up fairly quick.

DUMPSTER DIVING

Dumpster diving or digging through a person's trash can will be a surprising topic for most of you. In most states, whether it's Law Enforcement, a Private Investigator, or simply just a random citizen, digging through the trash can of a random person is completely legal.

The legal reasoning behind this is that when a person discards "trash" into a trash can, they are waiving their right to an "expectation of privacy". In other words, you have told the world that not only do you no longer have interest in keeping these things, there is also an implication that this "trash" can end up in the hands of anyone.

Trust me when I say this, digging through the trash of

others is a highly-practiced method by investigators. It seems a bit outdated, but there's no better way to discover essential details about a person's life than in their trash.

SURVEILLANCE

Surveillance comes in many shapes and sizes. Whether it's performed by private citizens, licensed Private Investigators, or Law Enforcement, it is happening at all times and in all places.

In my experience, though surveillance makes up the majority of cases with private investigation, most investigators attempt to avoid this type of work. It's very time-consuming and straight up boring. To add to that, most experienced investigators know that even when they catch that "golden nugget" they were looking for, it sometimes rarely matters to insurance companies or courts. Nevertheless, surveillance is a great way to obtain details about a person, their lifestyle, their associates, and their general mannerisms in regard to the eye of the public.

Whether licensed or unlicensed, surveillance is somewhat of a gray area in terms of legality. Yes, insurance companies and law firms are within their legal rights to hire third-party Investigators to conduct surveillance on an individual or company. However, legally speaking, anyone can do this due to the law regarding "public view". This essentially states that any information observed within view of the public is fair game. The "expectation of privacy" explanation comes back into play for surveillance. Are you granted the expectation of privacy while conducted business in the view of public? Generally, no. What about if you're within a residence with an open window? Then it gets a bit trickier, and though I will leave legal advice to someone that can legally give it, I will say that, "if you have to question it, it's probably not good".

Law firms and insurance companies hire third-parties for two reasons; It transfers most liability to the company/investigator that they hired in the event that something is conducted out of statute, and a more important reason, they hire third-parties to remain unbiased to the facts that are obtained during an investigation. If law firms or insurance companies conduct investigations on behalf of their client, OF COURSE, they want to receive the most detrimental facts for their case. This can quickly become a conflict of interest.

Experienced Surveillance Investigators are very smart at what they do. If you're traveling, it will never be the vehicle directly behind yours. Surveillance is conducted from a distance. The farther, the better. In addition, Surveillance Investigators typically have a general idea of the route that will be traveled by whom they are following. Main roadways between the target's home, work, favorite place to shop, etc. This pre-surveillance research is important in case an investigator loses their target at a traffic light or in heavy traffic.

Another device to be familiar with are GPS trackers. The legality of using a GPS tracker on someone's vehicle varies from state to state. Regardless of the laws surrounding the use of these devices, they can be found online for very cheap. It's a tool that anyone can purchase from the internet, stick to the underside of a vehicle, and monitor from their computer. In my expertise, I have only known a few Investigators to use them. For the same reason that they're legal to use in many states is the same reason investigators don't invest in them. The legal reasoning behind supporting the use of them is that a vehicle is already in "public view", which is a very legal method of observation. Though a GPS tracker may be more convenient, essentially it can't provide any more information that a human could provide.

Aside from investigators, law enforcement, or ill-willed citizens, there is also the element of electronic surveillance. Living in the 2020s, most people would assume that most places have surveillance surrounding their establishment. You would really be surprised how many places do not. Though, there are many that still do. It's best to assume that anywhere you go in public, you are being recorded by some type of surveillance system. Whether that's a traffic light, a convenience store at the corner of an intersection, or outside of a government building. Electronic surveillance is becoming more predominant throughout the country.

PREVENTATIVE HUMINT MEASURES

VEHICLES

There is absolutely no way to prevent an individual from obtaining Human Intelligence about you. However, there are ways to minimize the amount of information someone is likely to observe.

Your vehicle is an extension of your home. As I previously discussed, there are many, many clues about your family and yourself enclosed within that four-wheel machine.

For starters, it's crucial to remove all identifiable

information from your vehicle. This includes stickers, initials, favorite sports' teams, etc. Most importantly, remove any work badge you may have having from the rear-view mirror. Convenience is not a good excuse to parade your personal information around. Keep in mind, this is the same vehicle you take to your local shopping center. Multiple people will walk past it in the small time you're purchasing items. Why roll the dice with giving out information when you can simply remove it until needed?

But what about your license plate? Great question! Each state differs when it comes to the availability in researching a stranger's license plate. Even if your state doesn't allow this (even for Private Investigators), your tag still gives off a bit of information, like your state and county. Also, though your license plate number may only be ran by law enforcement agencies in your state, it's still an identifiable code to you. What I mean by that is that if you drive a very common vehicle and someone is currently looking for you, without your license plate number, it becomes a bit harder. Imagine you drive a white Toyota Camry and you're parked in a large parking lot with seven other white Toyota Camrys? The search becomes difficult. Though, if a Surveillance Investigator can identify you by your tag number, it turns a rough day into an easy one.

With all of that being said, I would suggest to back your vehicle into parking spots whenever possible. If you don't currently practice this, it may seem weird or annoying at first. Trust me, you'll get used to it just like anything, and it gives just a tiny bit of security while you're not around.

In general, it's a great practice to take alternative routes to work each day. Have no pattern, simply mix it up.

SPEAKING

One of my favorite acronyms is "KISS", which means, "Keep It Simple, Stupid". In other words, keep the information you verbally give out to a minimum. Many people have a problem with volunteering too much information to others, especially strangers. This is the primary goal of the Social Engineer. Keep your conversations to the point, give only needed information, and go from Point (A) to Point (B) as quickly as possible.

Of course there are times to elaborate during your conversation. If you're a salesperson and you "keep it simple", you will lose a good bit of sales. Each situation and each person create a different scenario for you to react to. Even when you "keep it simple", ensure you're not giving out personal information to someone that doesn't necessarily need it. Your address? The type of vehicle you drive? The city you were born? Ask yourself, "why is this needed"? The best way to practice minimizing the type of information you give out is to listen to how others speak. Make mental notes on the type of information they're unknowingly giving to you? Was all of that information needed? Which dots can you connect with that type of information? The more aware you become of how others speak, the more aware you will become about how you speak.

DOCUMENTS

Whether you're at your workplace or home, the best practice for preventing information from getting into the wrong person's hands is by shredding all documents. What may seem like an annoyance truly isn't much work at all. Keeping the "pulling the thread" method in mind, a document that may not seem to have important details to you can easily be helpful to another individual. Document shredders are inexpensive and can save you a lot of damage in the long run.

OPEN-SOURCE INTELLIGENCE (OSINT)

WHAT IS OPEN-SOURCE INTELLIGENCE?

Open-Source Intelligence (OSINT) is the process of obtaining information about a person or group through social media, search engines, and public records. Open-Source Intelligence is one of the easiest and most thorough ways to research a person or corporation in the technology-driven age.

Unfortunately, anyone with a Google search engine or Facebook account automatically believes they're a "natural investigator". Sites like Google and Facebook have surely helped the research/investigative community, but unfortunately, this couldn't be further from the truth.

During this chapter, we'll go over the basics of Open-Source Intelligence, easy tools to utilize, the legalities surrounding this type of research, and ways to suppress the type of information you have floating around on the web.

EXAMPLES OF OPEN-SOURCE

SOCIAL MEDIA

These days, Social Media tends to be the #1 go-to spot for finding someone, or finding information about someone. Social evolution has pushed the majority of the world to volunteer their face, personal details, and life's ups and downs to the rest of the world. Though it's surely not a perfect place for obtaining information, it can be very resourceful for someone attempting to gain specific information from a person.

RELATIONSHIP STATUS

On social media sites, it only takes a few seconds to realize if someone is in an active relationship or not. The issue with this is that each member of a relationship share this level of privacy once they announce their bond to the rest of the world. In other words, if one member of a relationship has a secured social media page but the other does not, investigators and hackers can used the unsecured members page as a backdoor. As most couples do, there will shared photos in specific locations, tagged statuses or comments, etc. Having a private page from strangers on the net is a team effort.

WORKPLACE

As many do, some individuals will list their workplace on their social media page. Though this can have advantages if you're deep into business networking and marketing, but there's always a downfall. As previously mentioned, each piece of information you give out risks just a bit more security of your personal life. With the name of a workplace, an individual can determine where you travel each day, where you park your vehicle, or maybe even which time you're supposed to arrive and leave. In addition, a complete stranger can pretext your workplace with your name for unethical reasons.

COLLEGE/SCHOOL

You may think that listing the college or high school you attended can be completely irrelevant to a stranger on the internet. This is very untrue. Countless times I have used this tab to pinpoint where a person originated from. If you're a person that moved across the country, whether it was to take a far-away position, or because you're simply just a military spouse that was forced to move, knowing your hometown college or high school can open a brand new door for strangers out there. Not only can it help social engineers match your profile to an online database, but it can also help them determine easy security questions like, "name your high school mascot".

PLACE YOU LIVE

When you stumble across someone on the internet, essentially, they could live anywhere. The more common there name is, the harder they are to find. From an outsider's point of view, you are somewhat like a "needle in a haystack". However, when you list the state, city, or county that you live in on your social media page, it's like putting a magnifying glass over your head. This mistake has been extremely useful for someone like me in the private investigation field when I need to track someone down.

For instance, let's take a name like "David Smith". How many David Smiths are there in the United States? According to the former site, www.HowManyOfMe.com, there are over 35,000 people in the United States with that name. Again, it's a needle in a haystack.

Now let's say that this specific David Smith lists the small town that he lives in on his social media page. That 35,000 turns into less than 20. Less than 20 is manageable, 35,000 is not. From that point, the individual seeking to find David Smith will use other identifiable information to narrow that 20 down to 1.

FRIENDS/FAMILY

It never fails. Individuals are always, somehow, some way connected to their relatives. This is even more true for their friends due to the fact that, in rare cases, people cut ties from their family, completely. A good tactic to play anonymity through social media sites is to not use a last name on your profile, or use a completely false name. It's true, this can become quite the obstacle for locating someone with ease. However, just like anything, there's always another route to take. In this instance and something I've done many times before is to dissect each page to find a common last name. If you examine their list of friends or group of friends that like or comment on each post or photo, you'll eventually find their given last name. For someone to remain anonymous with a false last name, they would have to convince all of their family members to do the same. This is not likely whatsoever. From there, you dig deeper into the pages of their relatives for that golden nugget of someone naming your target in a photo. For example, "here's John and I at the wedding". Bam, first name and last name solved! If this method fails, there's another to take it's place. For instance, maybe you don't find a photo with this person's first name, but you find a local court record with them listed as a witness on a relative's case. Same conclusion, different method. Just like any resolution, investigations require the accumulation and analysis of data. If you dig deep enough, you will likely find exactly what you're looking for.

LOCATION TAGS & HASHTAGS

I used to play a game where I would challenge myself to discover every possible thing about a random stranger by simply walking past them. Not only have I challenged myself, but I have taught many people how to do the same. Essentially, this entire book is a resource for tools to use when doing this, but location tags can make this task very simple, especially given the right personality of your target. Events, tourist areas, and nice places all have one thing in common; people love to take photos while they visit or pass through. Additionally, many of those people like to tag the location that they're currently at or have visited. With a simple search of that area on any social media app, you can can view photos or videos taken, and even filter down to the most recent. You would be surprised how easy this task is. Just like anything, results may vary with specific situations. For instance, if a person is simply traveling on foot to their bus stop, the likelihood of them posting and tagging a social media photo is quite slim. However, a person is out on a night drinking, celebrating a birthday, or visiting a famous location, the likelihood of coming across a tagged photo increases significantly. It's small tactics like this that can quickly open doors you didn't even know existed. My advice to individuals that prefer to tag locations on their photos or videos is to, of course have a private profile. Secondly, I would suggest waiting until you have left that location to post a photo or video with a tag. Just in case someone is seeking you in real-time, it's safer to return home before making such a post.

With that being said, hashtags are used exactly the same way. As an example, let's say surveillance is being conducted on a target that is visiting Atlanta, Georgia for a weekend getaway. During their stay, if you're constantly researching hashtags similar to #Atlanta or #DowntownATL, it's quite possible you will stumble across a photo of them. This doesn't even necessarily mean that it was posted to their account, it could have been posted on a friend or significant other's account. Of course, this method tends to work a lot easier with outgoing, tech-savvy people. Nevertheless, it's another tool in a very large toolbox. The more you practice, the quicker you'll know what to use, when to use it, and the success rate of each use.

Now, let me pause and ask a question. In this paragraph, why did I use Atlanta as an example? I could have picked any city of any state, or any country. However, I picked Atlanta for reference. Ask yourself why I did that. Is it because I live in Atlanta?

Do I live in Georgia? Did I just come back from vacation in Atlanta? Am I leaving for vacation to Atlanta tomorrow? There's no such thing as coincidence. It's imperative that you're always analyzing WHAT people say, but most importantly, WHY they said it. Moving forward, program your mind to start thinking like this.

PHOTOS OF YOUR HOME ADDRESS

This one is a given. It's not-so-smart to post the number of your physical address. This is not because it's exactly harmful per se to have your address publicly displayed, but for investigative reasons. Let's say there is someone out there researching you through public databases, but they can't determine if they're viewing a list of your information or someone else with the same name. Well, this group of information would include an address, and if they're now aware of your address, they can conclude that the person they are viewing is, in fact, you. Additionally, it's a better practice to keep your address safeguarded as best as possible, especially if you have small children. Any twist or turn you can throw in the way of someone attempting to violate you makes it that much harder for them.

ONLINE QUESTIONNAIRES

Online questionnaires are my absolute favorite peace of information when it comes to conducting research on a person or attempting to locate them. This is even more so true for the average social engineer. Thousands of times a day, naive-minded individuals fill out online questionnaires that can be viewed publicly. Out of those thousands, how many people are actively being pursued or investigated. There are no good statistics to support an approximate number, however, even one unlucky person can be a travesty.

Though these questionnaires ask questions that appear to be harmless, they're far from it. Not only are advertisers and social media companies collecting and selling your information, investigators and social engineers are now given a glimpse into your life. Where did you go to high school? What was the name of your first pet? These are also known as security questions that are used to access accounts, including bank accounts. Aside from the potential harm just in that, there have been many times I, myself, have come across completed online questionnaires from a person I was conducting surveillance on. Using answers from questions about which town you're currently in or where your favorite place to shop is located can lead a person directly to you. In many cases, it has. Though I recommend never playfully filling these questionnaires out, if you feel absolutely compelled to, at least ensure that your social media profile is private to outsiders. It always tend to be the smallest of careless pieces of information that open the biggest doors for social engineers.

DATABASES

Databases are typically a starting point for most investigators and/or social engineers. Databases that contain Personally Identifiable Information (PII) are either private or public. As public information continues to be bought, sold, and shared, there is somewhat of a gray area for which type of information the average person can get their hands on.

The most common information that are found on these types of database include:

SOCIAL SECURITY NUMBERS

For the most part, a social security are primarily found on private databases that require special access. However, this is not always the case. Social security numbers can still be found on cases in some courts, and some paid online databases do provide these for a fee. As I said, there is somewhat of a gray area.

DATE OF BIRTH

In my personal opinion, having someone's date of birth is a lot more dangerous than having their social security number. Many people believe the privacy of their social security number is the gold standard, but just as much damage can be done with a person's birthday, and it's far easier to acquire. As I mentioned in the previous section, someone can determine your birth date by asking simple and harmless questions. For example, if your birthday was the amount of money in your account, how rich would you be? You'd be surprised how many people carelessly answer this question for public consumption.

PHONE NUMBERS

Any phone number that you have used, paid for, or been within a plan of will link back to you. These links aren't always in black in white. For instance, if someone researches your name, your parent's phone number may be attached to your available information. Any time you sign up for something online, whether it's paid or free, your phone number associated with the sign-up may or may not be sold to other companies. My suggestion is to be picky about the type of information you give out. It's nearly impossible to prevent the transfer of your personal information, but every little bit helps.

HOME ADDRESS

Any place you have received mail to, rented, purchased, or paid utilities for will be linked back to you. Again, the address itself may not be harmful to you. From an investigator's point of view, the investigator would know each city and county you have resided in. From there, they would research you further through public court records in those cities and counties. It's like pulling a thread.

FAMILY TREE

Most private databases provide family member-linking. If you're searched, your family and close friends will more-than-likely populate as well. Sometimes, the database will show the relation between each party and yourself. This could be due to many factors. Court records may have linked you, living in the same household, using the same phone plan, etc.

VEHICLE TAG

Most states restrict the access of driver and vehicle information, however, private databases still provide most of this information. In addition, many data companies now provide users with vehicle whereabouts. Through the many ways to accumulate photo and video data from information brokers, these software companies can provide information from locations that a specific vehicle plate was spotted via photo or video. Paranoia aside, it's typically a better practice to back into a parking spot. Without this service being used, vehicle tags still give out basic information about yourself.

CRIMINAL & CIVIL RECORDS

Private databases are typically hit or miss when it comes to finding an individual's court cases. However, courts are extremely accurate. We'll discuss courts shortly. Private databases are a very good starting point to direct a person to a specific court to search in person, or even on a county court's online public database.

This is just an example of the majority of information that can be found on public or private databases. For some people, there is more. For others, there is less. This is why it's imperative for an investigator to be proficient in many different research tools, not just one.

PRIVATE INVESTIGATION/ATTORNEY DATABASES

When you work in the industry as an attorney, licensed private investigator, debt collection agency or similar, you may have access to private databases with personally identifiable information. This type of information is top tier and these databases are even used my almost all law enforcement agencies. Aside from the professional license requirement and monthly paid-subscription, these companies utilize third-party compliance companies to conduct a physical inspection of the location where the software will be used. Given that there are many laws regarding the use of this type of information, with FCRA guidelines being the most common, it's imperative that this type of information is secured and stored safely.

PAID ONLINE SUBSCRIPTIONS

Similar to databases that are available for professional licenses, paid online subscriptions for so-called background checks are a dime a dozen. Unfortunately and fortunately, there are a few differences. For starters, they're not regulated in terms of safeguarding information or even the accuracy of information. Secondly, yes, the accuracy of information is subpar in comparison to professional databases. Though I have used these online methods from time-to-time even while having a professional source, the outcome is wildly different.

HOW IS THIS INFORMATION BOUGHT/SOLD?

Data brokering is one of the biggest international businesses as of today. Information about individuals becomes very valuable to data companies or companies that are attempting to market a product or service to a specific type of demographic. You see this effort every single day. How did Google know that about me? How did Facebook know I wanted pizza? It's unfortunately to a level that is unavoidable in today's standards. So where are they getting this information? Well, data brokers can retrieve your information from many, different locations. Whether it's public records, online scraping, utility bills, or something random you signed up for on the internet, rest assured, it will be collected and sold to someone else.

SEARCH ENGINES

INDEXED SEARCHES

Indexed searches are simply a collection of information that is indexed within a large database to spew top results in a quick manner. AKA Google. Though you still can't find everything or everyone through a simple Google search, you can still get pretty far due to their high volume of information and their indexing features. Many times in the past, I have found information on Google that I couldn't necessarily find on a professionally licensed database. For example, if a database doesn't show familial relationships between adults, a posted obituary from the past few years surely will. Any efficient search requires the use of multiple tools.

REVERSE IMAGE SEARCHES

Aside from Google's well-known reverse image search, there are other competitors in the market that provide the same service. A reverse image search is the use of an uploaded photo to find other photos to match the specifics. As technology soars and daily information is being added to engines like Google, the results are becoming more in-depth. Now in 2024, we're starting to see better results when it comes to uploading the photo of a face and having the search engine tell us who it is. Though only celebrities are really making these results successful, it's only a matter of time before you'll be able to find your name by the search of your face. As of current, if you search a known profile photo from someone's social media page, the results are approximately 50% reliable. This is because profile photos are also public photos and are indexed through the databases of search engines. My suggestion is to keep the least amount of photos public as possible.

PUBLIC RECORDS

Public records are referred to as documents or

information that are readily available for the public to view or inspect. Public records, in my opinion, are the best source for researching another person or entity. The reliability is of the highest standard given that the information is obtained and kept by government offices, and the sources available and typically free to access. There are many types of offices or sites for different types of public records, but we will go over the most common and easiest to use.

COURTS

Court records are such a beautiful source when it comes to researching a person. Prior to research, it's important to know which county of which state your target has lived, visited, etc. As of 2024, most counties across the country provide online databases you can search for records. Though, sometimes it requires actually visiting a court or submitting an open records request to the County Clerk's Office to receive personally identifiable information for verification purposes. All counties across the country have Public Access Terminals located within the courthouse to conduct research on individuals or entities. These computers do provide personally identifiable information. Court records are primarily broken down into two categories: Criminal and Civil cases.

Aside from the dates, times, law enforcement agency, suspect, and charges, criminal records provide a lot more about a person. Let's use an example of a basic traffic citation. This citation will be scanned and uploaded to the public access terminal in the courts. So just because you were cited for a basic traffic offense, any average person can walk into the courthouse and obtain your current address, the make and model of your vehicle, your date of birth, your phone number, your height and weight, the next time you will be present at the courthouse, and sometimes even your social security number. All of that is pulled from a simple citation and this is even without being convicted.

Civil cases typically have a lot less personally identifiable information, however, where they lack in specifics, they gain additional types of information. Civil cases can be anything from a divorce to a lawsuit. By browsing through these types of records, you can find close relatives that are mentioned in cases, witnesses, a financial affidavit of your assets, your current job and how much you make a month, your significant relationship and their name, the name of your children, and much, much more.

As you can tell, just by someone knowing the county where you reside can be problematic. I think it's safe to say that the majority of us have had at least one speeding ticket, so keep this in mind. In addition, my suggestion is to never give your phone number to law enforcement for a traffic citation or arrest. This information is not required and the entire public will have it within days.

Again, the least amount of information you put out into the world, the better.

TAX ASSESSOR

The Tax Assessor's Office of each county throughout

the United States holds tax and real estate information regarding every piece of property. For the most part, almost all of these records are available online as of 2024. A simple address or owner name search will provide details of an owner, previous owners, contact information, and sometimes even a blueprint of the home and property. There are many instances, in which, this type of information is useful. If you're trying to figure out where a subject lives within a county, you can simple plug their name in to the site. Another example would be if a person were being surveilled and they continued visiting a home with unknown owners, you could simply plug the address in to establish a connection between the surveilled party and the homeowner.

Maybe there is a silver lining to renting instead of owning, after all.

BUSINESS LICENSE SEARCH

For each state, there is a search engine to research current and past business licenses. This is typically found under a state's Secretary of State's Office. If you're attempting to find the owner or officers of an establishment, simply plug the business name info the state's search tool. In addition, you can search by an owner's name to see if they're currently operating under a business license within the state. When you access these records, there will be documentation describing when the business was started, the initial and current address of establishment, and anyone legally tied to the business in an operating capacity. I some cases, you can find direct emails and home addresses from these records. Like many start-up companies, a person may initially register their business from home. This record of an address now exists forever.

My suggestion for anyone in the circumstance of creating a new business from home is to use a third party service for a mailing address within the state. The reasons I wouldn't suggest using a Post Office Box is because most states do not allow a business to be registered to a P.O. Box.

LOCATION SERVICES

If there's one thing that media companies love to know about you, it's your location. For obvious purposes, marketing ads become a lot easier if you location is known. However, keeping your location turned on with your devices opens a back door to social engineers or any other type of people trying to locate you.

SOCIAL MEDIA SITES

As previously mentioned, it's a better practice to not tag the locations of where you travel and to keep your location as private as possible. With growing technology and new apps hitting the market daily, it's important to be weary of how your location is used. Though many apps give up a bit of privacy, I will use only one to give an example. In my career, I used Snapchat on a few occasions to pinpoint the location of another person. When I say pinpoint, I mean the exact house they were in at that present moment. So you must ask yourself if keeping your location on is even necessary at all. Yes, it's very convenient to search a location and get directions though a search engine. In that case, simply turn your location ON, then back OFF when you're finished. This is only one of many ways that your location may be used against you.

PHOTOGRAPH METADATA

How can a photo reveal your location? Well you see... when you take a photo with your location services turn to the ON position, metadata is attached to every photo you take during that time. This means your photo details now include the exact grid coordinates of where you were. This can become even more of an issue if you're trying to keep the location of your home private. Again, safeguarding as much as possible is always the best answer. If you're an individual that likes to keep the location services of your devices turned ON, at least turn them off while you take photos. Every little bit helps toward privacy.

ARE OSINT SEARCHES LEGAL?

Are Open-source Intelligence searches legal, and if

not, how can someone navigate around that? An easy answer for that is yes and no. Though open-source research is completely legal and open to the public, there's a gray area when it comes to what you're planning on doing with that research. Most industry professionals will tell you that open-source searches are legal if they're not backed by malicious purposes or acts and I concur with that answer. Each state has different statutes when it comes to OSINT or acts that are similar, but regardless, these tend to fall on the civil side, not criminal. What I'm not saying right now is that you may not be held criminally liable for acts that come from OSINT searches. I am simply saying OSINT is legal and to use it legally and wisely.

PREVENTATIVE OSINT MEASURES

Throughout this book thus far, I have been discussing preventative measures to prevent open-source intelligence research being conducted on yourself.

If you can handle legal situations without law enforcement or using the court system, do so. This will amount to less times that your name and personal information populate on public or private databases.

If your paranoia is higher than the average person, rent places to live instead of buying a home.

If you partake in social media accounts, keep your information minimal and private.

When giving out a number to a source you do not 100% trust, use a burner phone or download a burner phone application that will allow you to use random numbers. In addition, you can purchase temporary phone numbers that work directly from your regular phone number.

Unless necessary, always keep the location on your media devices turned to the OFF position.

Again, and I will repeat this a million times throughout this book, but EVERY little bit helps.

Remember, as a former investigator, there have been many times that I simply got lucky by finding one piece of information by accident. This opened a brand new door and turned an unsuccessful case, successful.

If asked, many investigators will agree with that example.

UNDERSTANDING COMMUNICATION

In general, communication is the most important factor when trying to persuade your listener with your belief system. As a social engineer, your belief system requires extracting information from the listener. Therefore, it's imperative to be the master of understanding how each type of person communicates, and how to communicate in their language to obtain your wants and needs. Let me ask you a question. How many times have you received a phone call or email from someone with broken English? What is your first thought? It's more-than-likely that they're from another country and you perceive this as an attempted scam.

Now what if that same person was a master in the English language? What if it was physically in person? Let's say you're a soft-spoken person so they match that tone and don't make you anxious as you generally would be.

Let's say this person starts referencing some of your same interests and hobbies.

You're not sure why this person is prying for information, but you're starting to justify giving it to them in your head because they're just so likable. Let's throw another curve ball and say they're attractive and flirtatious with you. Now how likely are you to answer the questions they're asking you?

This person has no interest in you, they have simply mastered the basics of Social Engineering. They picked up few clues about yourself and used it against you to speak the exact language you needed to hear to obtain their wants.

In my book, *Sell Your Mind: NLP, Business Psychology, & 5MSM*, I break down each type of person when it comes to keeping a conversation, as well as specific communication traits and tactics. That information is not necessary for basic social engineering.

Everyone, without any formal training, have the ability to become a master of social engineering and communication. Just as any subject, you learn the basics and build as you grow.

Take time for yourself and go to a book store or coffee shop. Watch people. Observe their communication patterns. Do they like to be up close and personal or do they need distance? Do they like to be touched or no? Do they seem private or cut off? What's their current mood look like? Can you identify anything else about their life by viewing their clothing, body, or personal items?

Compare and contrast people against each other. The

more you learn how to categorize targets, the easier it becomes to master conversations with strangers on the fly. Just remember, you're only comparing the individuals that showed up to the location that you're at. This doesn't include the religiously homebodies that never leave the house.

WHAT IS NLP?

Neuro-linguistic Programming is the communication-based approach of programming neurological responses and human behaviors with language models. This practice involves understanding personality types, thought patterns, neurological triggers, body language, and a variety of methods involving communication. NLP primarily interacts with the subconscious mind as it uses three different approaches to embed or suggest ideas; Auditory, Visual, and Kinesthetic. The practice of NLP allows a practitioner to become proficient in levels of persuasion, rapport, and communication, Users of of NLP become more self-aware of communication tactics and the complexity of personal traits. These techniques have been found useful on applying to others, as well as programming self-help techniques through muscle memory for the user.

Neuro-linguistic Programming was created in the 1970s by Richard Bandler, who practiced psychotherapy, and John Grinder, a practicing linguist. Since its creation, NLP has evolved its methodology and framework, and is used in many different settings across the world. NLP is primarily known for it's role in the self-help field and has become a multi-billion dollar industry.

COMMUNICATION BREAKDOWN

Communication is the entire meaning behind Neuro-linguistic Programming. How to quickly and efficiently communicate or suggest your ideas into another person's subconscious space. With that being said and as I have mentioned before, there is no need to dial back into the creation of this methodology and how it has evolved. Knowing and practicing these methods is everything that you will need to change your success rate overnight. Now, let's get STRAIGHT to the point.

To understand how to proficiently communicate to others, whether it's employees or potential clients, you need to first understand the rate at which communication is intercepted and from which area it comes from. Studies have show that communication from one person to the other is broken down as so:

Body language is conveyed at around 55%.

The tone of your voice comes across between 35 and 40%.

Your spoken words rate ONLY between 5 and 10%.

Crazy, right? This means that the tone, in which you speak, outweigh your choice of words by approximately eight times. This makes a lot of sense if you think about it, right? You can easily tell if someone is angry, depressed, or happy simply by the tone of their voice. Make sure you remember this breakdown when you begin to put NLP techniques into play. The nicest words imaginable can quickly be turned into a client walking away and a BAD review, simply because you forgot the interpretation rates.

Keeping in mind how IMPORTANT tone is while conveying a message, keeping an inflection in your voice will help to keep your listener interested. If you've ever dealt with a teacher that keeps the same language tone throughout the entire class, you know exactly what I mean. It will quickly put you to sleep. Speaking of "quickly", you should always get to the point. Not in the sense that it's a race to get your words out, but people will lose interest if you're beating around the bush of needed-information. Be clear. Be precise.

Here is something to begin practicing; Let's say we're grading our tone level on a scale from one to ten. During your normal conversation you will range from a two to a six, just to keep the listener interested. However, when you use exclusive terms like, "give" or "hurry", boost your tone up to an eight, maybe a nine. This will create an anchoring effect in the listener's mind.

Moving on, body language accounts for approximately 55% of communication. Though there are many suggested techniques that work for the subject of body language, we will primarily focus on these during the instruction on Mirroring.

A great rule of thumb while using body language is that you need to keep fluidity. As you can tell from learning personality types is that some people like their distance, while some prefer you up close and personal. One easy way to spot that is by watching their eye movements. When speaking of GENERAL body language, I specifically mean where they tend to keep their eyes positioned, on average. This has nothing to do with moving left, to right, up, and down after each spoken phrase.

So, if the opposing person generally keeps their eyes positioned upward, it means they like to have their space. Make sure you're not crowding these people. What I'm NOT saying is that you should speak to them from across the room. I'm NOT saying that. Just an arm's distance or so.

With people that stare almost straight into the ground, you may need to adjust closer to them, similar to a sports huddle-up.

It's imperative to remember the breakdown of how communication is divided up. If you spend too much time worrying about precise wording, you may just lose the person you're speaking to. Burn this information into your methods. Body language, Tone, Words. In that order. Over and over again.

DECEPTIVE PRACTICES & SIGNS;

Next, we'll go a few deceptive practices and signs of of the common social engineer. Just as anything, it's imperative to practice until it becomes part of your muscle-memory, then expand your knowledge to deeper subjects or deeper context.

DIVERSIONARY TACTICS

As mentioned above, communication is just a steady flow of information going in and out of the mind. Our minds and essentially the entire world around us work as patterns. Just as 1, 2, 3, and a, b, c. Let me ask you this. Have you ever known what you were going to answer to a question before a person finished asking it? I assume, yes, as most have. This is because our brains are not only trained on patterns, but specific languages, questions, remarks, etc. To break that cycle, a diversionary tactic can be deployed. Here's another example. I have used this example many times because it's fitting and extremely normal. So, imagine you get into your vehicle, reach for the seat belt, buckle it, then start the vehicle just as you every single day, multiple times a day. This is a pattern. Your mind has added this to your muscle memory. You can do this without thinking, can you not?

So, what if when you went to reach for the seat belt, there was no seat belt present? You reached for and grabbed air. This would cause a disoriented pause in pattern for your brain. This is approximately 5 seconds of time, in which, our minds are very vulnerable. Keep that 5-second pause in mind.

Now apply the seat belt scenario to any other scenario in your life. If you're a front desk employee of a large corporation, your position consists of patterns. These patterns are your daily tasks with a few variables here and there. You know which type of person will call or approach your desk. You know along the lines of what they will say and ask. You know what your programmed responses are with very few variables.

Now, what if that employee receives a call and the person on the other ends says, "I like the color of your dress today", and hangs up?

The front desk employee's mind will freeze. This is not part of the script. The brain uses all of it's awareness to now focus in on this one, weird occurrence. Does it not? This is where the mind is very vulnerable to attacks.

Let's go back to the seat belt and vehicle scenario. While buckling your seat belt as you always do, if a red car passed in front of you, you would at least know those two facts. Car and red.

What if you reached and your seat belt was not there? When the brain freezes, do you think you would remember the car or the fact that it was red? More-than-likely not.

Therefore, educating yourself on how to respond to diversions can be imperative, not only in a professional setting, but in your personal life as well. Small things matter.

Why would a hacker attempt to hack your computer, when they could simply start a small fire in the ashtray outside of your office and pass you while you run out to extinguish the burning? That's only one of a million simple diversionary tactics. What if a two-man team are attempting to bypass your security guard at the front desk and one fakes a heart attack? The second person has about one to two minutes to accomplish what he came for, and trust me, that is long enough.

Just remember, this can be one of countless scenarios that play through. Don't ever think that your company is not important enough to get hacked because you'll never be able to know everyone's wants, nor their reasons.

EYE ACCESSING CUES

Do we have the capability of reading eye patterns? Yes, absolutely. What we don't have the capability of doing is reading the mind. At least not yet as for today's standards. However, reading eye patterns allows us to understand the direction of thought, in which, a person is thinking. This is called Eye Accessing Cues.

Having a grasp on how to read someone's eye patterns can allow us to understand whether a person is thinking of sights, sounds, actual events that have taken place, or events that they're currently creating on the spot. Essentially, this gives a reader the power to determine if the person speaking is being truthful or not.

Before we go over each eye movement, let's discuss some basic exceptions to watch out for.

Though most speakers can be monitored from the

same layout of patterns that will be given to you, there are a few people that will display all of their readings in a reverse order. Instead of left, their direction will be right, instead of right their direction will be left. It has been said that this is primarily due to the differences in left and right-handed people, but there still aren't enough recorded studies to conclude that theory. In order to prevent reading a person incorrectly, it's always better to test the person near the beginning of the conversation. A great way to test a person's pattern direction is by asking simple questions like what color their vehicle is, or if the weather was sunny the day before.

When attempting to question another person while reading their eyes, it's imperative that your questions are clear and to the point. Because you're reading a person's direction of thoughts, you must ensure that the person is ONLY thinking about one thing. Of course there is no 100% solid way to prevent a person from thinking about hamburgers and hot dogs when you ask them about their vehicle, but by keeping your questions straight and to the point, you can limit

WHAT the speaker is supposed to think about.

EYE PATTERNS

There are six directions, in which, the eyes move during a conversation. Each direction carries a specific meaning, and can be traced back to the speaker's underlying message.

The six directions are; Visual Construction, Auditory Construction, Visual Remembered, Auditory Remembered, Kinesthetic, and Auditory Internal.

As I explain what each one means, do me a favor and visualize someone's face staring directly at yours.

My explanation will be based on what you see on that face, just so we can stay on the same page with lefts and rights.

Visual Remembered. When a person is asked to recall how something looks, they will look up and to the right as they visually remember.

Visual Construction. If a person asked to imagine something, just as I asked you to imagine the face, a person will look up and to the left. They are visually constructing the image.

Auditory Remembered. If asked to recall how a live concert sounded, a person will look to their middle-right. They are remembering the sounds of the concert.

Auditory Construction. If a person is asked what they think will be said during an important meeting, they will look to their middle-left. They are constructing the sounds of the dialogue.

Kinesthetic. If a person is asked about how they deeply feel on a subject, they will look to the bottom left. They are accessing their own feelings pertaining to the subject mentioned.

Auditory Internal. When a person looks to the lower right, they are having an internal dialogue with their self. This could be one of many reasons, but a well-known internal dialogue is self-motivation. Telling yourself, "you can do it", or "you're almost there, don't give up".

You may be asking yourself, "what if they look straight ahead"? Good question. No worries, all this means is that they're recalling something from their short term memory, and have no need to put much thought into the question. Allow some room for patience, and be more creative in your questions.

The observation of eye patterns can be used on or off the clock.

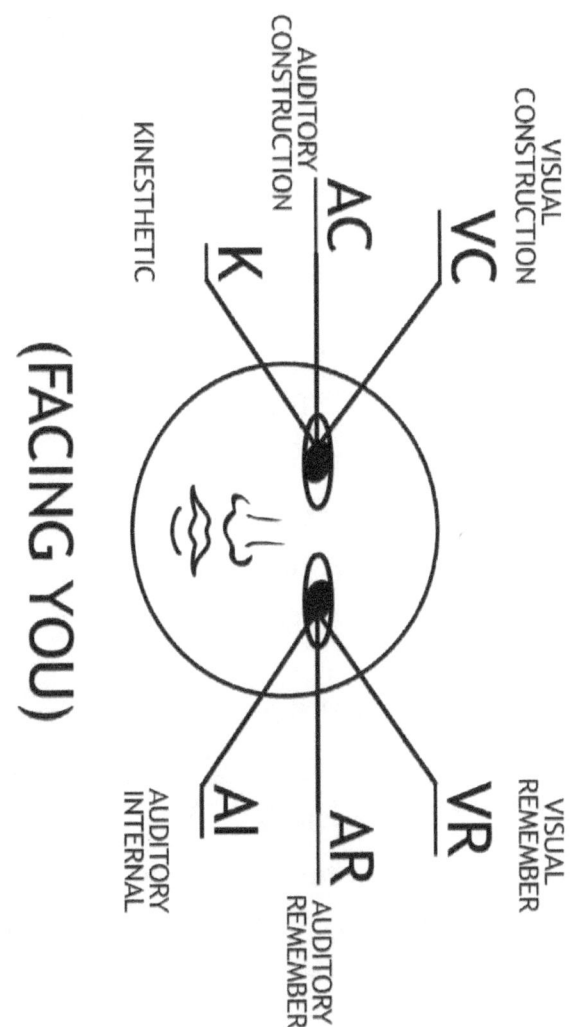

MIRRORING & PACING

Mirroring and pacing go hand-in-hand, though each can be used apart from each other, and work just as great. After we go over each technique, you'll be able to understand the basics, in which format and order they're used, and how to successfully deploy each.

MIRRORING

Mirroring is definitely one of the best known methods used in Neuro-Linguistic Programming, and can be found in many different sales training manuals throughout the world. Though mirroring is one of the absolute best ways to establish rapport with a prospect, it is also one of the riskiest.

What we're trying to accomplish by mirroring someone is to generate rapport from the other person by mirroring their movements. To look at this in a different light, imagine that the prospective client sees their actual words coming from YOUR body. You're creating that illusion by mirroring their moves. They're essentially staring into a mirror. This method causes the other person to feel as if you're someone to trust or confide in. There are a few ways to accomplish this, but let's examine the basic setup.

Let's say that you're sitting in a job interview that's for a position you've always dreamt of having. You need your future employer to insist that you're the person for this position. In order to do so, you'll need to prove that you're trustworthy and confident within only ten minutes or so.

Therefore, you begin to mirror the employer's movements, to inevitably have he or she view YOUR words coming from THEIR body. If they move their left arm, you will move your right, so on and so forth.

Here are a few things that we can mirror;

- Movement of body parts
- Speech tone
- Speech speed, and
- Emotions

While you're sitting across from this other person, after they make a move with, let's say their arm, make sure you wait a few seconds before you do the same movement. If you're too quick, the other person will be able to notice, and you'll completely blow your cover.

I have found that sometimes it is necessary to create a diversionary tactic. For example, if they cross their leg to the other side, bend forward and pretend to wipe something off of the table quickly while you're crossing your leg to the other side. This movement will ride right under their radar, and you'll go straight back to a mirrored image with them.

It's imperative that you're as covert as possible. It's better to mimic NO movements, than to mirror improperly and get caught doing so. As I said, if you get noticed, it's game over. On the other hand, if you practice and become successful and this method, it will easily reward you with much-needed rapport.

MIRRORING EXERCISE

The best way to practice mirroring is by actually mirroring each person that you encounter, EVEN if there is no desired result. However, a good tool to use for practicing this method is to make small movements into an actual mirror. This, of course, will not be aligned with how you actually mirror someone, because you can't set time delays of each movement. Yet, what we can discover by doing this is what types of mirrored movements look unnatural or too obvious. Keep in mind, the number one thing you want to avoid while mirroring is having the other person catch on to what you're doing.

PACING

To define the meaning of pacing, it's simply leading another person to a place you want them to be. This can be used verbally or physically.

Where do you want another person to be? In sales, that's a pretty simple answer; to the closing. So how do we use pacing to get someone there? Simple.

Let's first examine how this is used alongside

mirroring, so you can picture how the process works.

When mirroring another person's movements correctly, you will begin to establish a very strong bond with the opposite person. At this point, you can start making subtle movements outside of the mirror. Therefore, while completely mirroring a person's stance, move an arm or leg. If you're rapport is strong enough, the other person will subconsciously follow your lead. Their arm or leg will mirror yours. Now you are leading the mirrored movements. This is called "Pacing".

Why is this a good tactic? Well, for starters, it's a good testing method to test how strong your current rapport is. Secondly, in a physical sense, this would be a good method to lead your prospect to an item you want them purchase. Maybe you're a phone salesman and you would like them to purchase the high-end model cell-phone. You mirror their movements, establish strong rapport, now use the pacing method to lead them to the device. Yes, this example is a bit far-fetched, but not impossible.

Now that we understand the basic format of pacing, let's talk about how this can be used in speech.

So, the setup is to get in the prospect's zone, then lead them to yours.

How do we get in? First we must understand why you're even speaking to the person in the first place. For instance, if someone walks into the dealership that you work, they're probably unhappy with their current vehicle. At least to the point where they're browsing for another. So let's start there. When you're conversing with the prospect, you need to get in their zone. You need to share the discomfort that they're currently having with their vehicle. You need to mirror their current emotional state, and even add your own stories that relate to their exact problems. Once you're rapport is fully intact, it's time to lead them to their new vehicle.

I understand, this concept sounds so easy. The problem is, salesmen often skip by the first step and go straight into number two. In this scenario, no one will buy from you. Why? Because you haven't built their trust. You're not mirroring THEIR actions, so good luck having them subconsciously mirror YOURS.

Pacing can be used in multiple formats. As mentioned, it can be used with physical mirroring. For instance, you can mirror someone's physical movements, then use pacing to lead them into buying by simply using words. They're interchangeable. In addition, you may use this pacing technique during cold calls, and even in written out scripts.

Draw this simple process out on a piece of paper. Client, mirror, lead, sell. By seeing how easy this process is, you'll be able to master it's chain of events when dealing with potential clients. Every single person on every single day has to act the part of a salesperson. It doesn't matter if you're currently acting this way in a professional setting, or selling an idea to your significant during a conversation. We as humans, are always selling.

JAW DROP-SIMULATED SPEECH

There is a micro-expression I have observed over many years, and it's definitely my favorite due to it's level of accuracy. I suppose there's not an actual term for this observation, therefore, I'll just call it a Jaw Drop-simulated Speech. It's not a speech though, it's actually a lack of speech and more of a pause. Nevertheless, when I encounter someone through interviews or basic conversation that is being untruthful, they will do a specific movement with their mouth. If you look closely to the person, their jaw will unclench ever so slightly to where the teeth are no longer touching inside the mouth. You can see this by the slight lowering of the jaw. This is typically prompted by asking a question to the person, and especially an off-the-wall type of question that they could not have prepared for. The jaw of the individual will unlench while they pause to answer. Surprisingly, this is often with a closed mouth, not an open one. Through my research and understanding with neuro-linguistic programming and psychology, this is essentially a microexpression that simulates something that should be said and is not. Instead, there is a pause and jaw release while the person formulates the best possible answer. An untruthful one. Test this practice on family, friends, and strangers. You will be surprised with the results.

PLAYING DUMB

The smartest people in the world are masters at playing dumb. However, there are two types of people that play dumb: people that are clearly playing it on purpose, and those that are believable.

There are a few reasons why an individual will utilize this method around others, but the easiest way to explain it is that they want zero responsibility. This means, they want no responsibility for words or things they hear, they want no responsibility for helping others, and most importantly, they want no responsibility when it comes to blaming someone for something that went wrong. For the social engineer, playing dumb can give an edge because no one suspects the not-so-smart guy of the genius crime. Additionally to that, others tend to get very loose-lipped and negligent in their security practices around or with people that play dumb. In other words, they're never viewed as a threat. They go under the radar and natural defenses slowly come down.

HUMILITY

For most of us, we are very familiar with the term, "humility". When we think of this word, we think of being humble. Not being too good to associate our self with others. As a matter of fact, a humble lifestyle doesn't even reach the societal norm in comparison. Humility allows us to tear down the walls of self-pride, and send an invitation of critique and well-aimed humor toward ourselves.

When meeting someone new, it's very rare to meet their humbled side which, in return, can cause the other person to create a defensive posture until that person is fully understood.

Simply put, when using humility, this can cause an individual to gain trust with you easier. Of course this is a primary conversation goal for meeting any new stranger, this is even more so important for social engineers attempting to extract information from their target.

FRACTIONATION

Our next tactic is on fractionation, and I must say, this subject really sticks out. Though this method was not originally created for professional use or good intentions, it will most definitely suffice for the basic social engineer.

Fractionation derives from the scientific term, "fractionation", meaning the process of a single mixture broken down into two smaller parts.

In NLP, the concept is very much so the same. We will be breaking down an overall encounter into two smaller parts. In the psychology and NLP fields of study, this method's meaning is directly linked into seduction from one person to another. Obviously, this topic is specifically related to communication-type engineering. As you will be able to tell, our methods will be applicable to encounters between prospective clients, strangers, etc.

Due to the fact that all humans rely on the sense and understanding of patterns when it comes to anything, that definitely includes communication. When encountering a stranger, it is the goal of the speaker to be steadily convincing the listener to have trust and confidence in their words, while it's the primary goal to be skeptical of the speaker. So how does fractionation disrupt that pattern and establish quick rapport from one person to the other?

Well, let's say you're attempting to sell a stranger on an idea you have. Fractionation, being known for quick seduction in the field of psychology, can easily be used in a professional format. This method can be used in person, phone calls, or digital messages. However, remember that calls and digital messages lose the edge of communicating your idea without body language. With our main goal being to establish rapport as quickly as possible, this method has become one of the most proficient to use.

Let's imagine a setting, in which, you're about to begin a conversation with an absolute stranger. For the purpose of this book, you're intention is to sell an idea to that stranger.

You, of course, have to sell yourself first, correct? To sell yourself, it's going to require that you build the amount of trust necessary to sell before the stranger leaves the conversation. How do we do this?

After the initial "hellos" and "how are you doings", let's start a conversation about general information that's NOT related directly to the idea, ONLY indirectly. For instance, if you're trying to sell a new vehicle, make conversation about a trip. Create a few of these indirect statements, surrounding your product. Then link them all to that new shiny vehicle.

NOW, here is where fractionation is used. As I have mentioned, this term was born from the scientific phrase of separating a single mixture into two smaller parts. The overall mixture here will be the conversation, while the two smaller parts will be the highs and lows of the conversation.

The high of a conversation needs to be an uplifting

story about yourself. Something that creates an overall smile on the person's face. An alternative to this would be to ask the individual to tell you about an amazing time in their life. Let's say you asked them to describe their first Christmas morning and how they felt. I'm only using Christmas morning as an example, but it needs to be similar in nature.

The low of the conversation needs to be something tragic that has either happened to the person or yourself. This needs to generate a feeling of sadness. Thus, creating a roller-coaster of emotions in your listener. In regard to that trip you previously mentioned, speak about a serious accident you were involved in, or maybe how you lost a loved one that was driving a vehicle with terrible safety features.

Having established the roller-coaster effect within your brief conversation, two things will happen;

For one, the person's initial judgment and programmed thought pattern that resists salespeople will be shut down. Just as someone will sit down in a vehicle and grab for their seat-belt a million times in a row. On the million and first try, the seat-belt is no longer there. You disrupted the subconscious thought pattern that drivers have programmed into their mind. Now, you replace it with your idea, and that is obviously for them to trust you.

Secondly, this instantly creates a strong bond that is needed to sell that vehicle. No one is going to buy a vehicle from someone they do not trust, and let's face it, car salesmen aren't the most trustworthy kind. The reason they're perceived that way is because they spend too much time on pushing their product, and not enough time creating the bond. Fractionation expedites that bonding experience, and allows you to get back to informing the prospect about the sale.

GUT INSTINCT (INTUITION)

Most importantly than anything when it comes to spotting social engineering is to trust your guy instinct. I can't stress how important your intuition is when it comes to potential threats. There is a very good reason for that as well. See, our subconscious mind is constantly receiving and analyzing information from our surroundings, unlike our conscious mind. Whether it's picking up sounds from afar, observing microexpressions from another person, or anything, our conscious mind doesn't always pick this up. Regardless, our mind is collecting information and attempting to alert the conscious mind of any potential threats by using the nervous system. This is why sometimes you can literally feel an issue in your stomach, hence "gut instinct". Nine times out of ten, if you feel like something is wrong, it surely is. Investigate further.

SIX TYPES OF COMMON SOCIAL ENGINEERING ATTACKS

Each year, there are brand new social engineering methods created to fool and potentially harm others. In this day and age, it's imperative to be familiar with the basic types of attacks, whether they're in-person, digital, or simply over the phone. It's unfortunately shocking how many people are completely oblivious to the very basic types of attacks that are currently out there. It's also unfortunate that we need to arm ourselves with education to combat these people on a daily basis. Next, we'll go over the six basic types of social engineering attacks so you'll be well-prepared moving forward. Even if and when these types of attacks evolve into more elaborate schemes, you'll still be able to recognize and protect yourself.

PRETEXTING

Pretexting is the common denominator of every type of social engineering attack. Pretexting is the act of disguising a name, occupation, or intention to gain access to secured information. In other words, it's the art of pretending to be someone else. Yes, this is very much so an art-form in my opinion, and this is where creativity can go very far. This includes the use of fake documents, fake identification cards, and simply lying to individuals over the phone or in person.

Though I have used countless pretexts throughout my career, I will give you two specific disguises I used. One these were successful while the other was not.

In one scenario, I used the pretext of a delivery driver. I needed to verify if an individual was an occupant of an address on file I had for her. I had already conducted surveillance for one day and observed zero movement from the residence. Therefore, I needed to see if someone answered, and if so, if there appeared to be anyone else in the residence. The preparation for this scenario was very minimal. I simply grabbed a black cap, wrapped an empty box, and wrote the details on the outside of the packaging. Instead of writing this individual's details one the package, I wrote down a random name that I made up.

I finally walked to the front door and knocked a few times. Sure enough, the person I was looking for answered right away. I informed her that I was looking for "blah blah blah", and she replied, "sorry no, my name is "blah blah blah".

Not only did I receive physical confirmation, but I also confirmed her name. Easy day.

For those thinking of the hazard it would be for me to go back to my vehicle, then conduct a few more days of surveillance, you're right, it would be. Thankfully, this was in the parking lot of an apartment complex and I was well-hidden. Another option would have been to switch out vehicles if you're local, or switch to a rental if you're out of town. Each case is a bit different, so it's imperative to know as many tools as possible.

The second scenario was a pretty big let down because I put far more work into this pretext. For this pretext, I disguised myself as a contracted Traffic Monitor for the county I was in. To be honest, I am not sure that such occupation even exists, but oh well. I had a falsely constructed contract, a fake identification card, and even a fake work form that was halfway filled out. The reason I chose this pretext is because if you've ever conducted surveillance, you know that location is key. Having a home or business at the end of a dead end or out in a very rural area can become a nightmare pretty quickly. The residence for this scenario was in a small dead end of about three or so homes, then immediately capped with a stop sign that led to the main highway.

Eventually, the individual I was conducting surveillance on approached my vehicle. This isn't necessarily a rare thing, but when it occurs, your words and actions should be chosen wisely.

This man then knocks on my window and asks me what I was doing in his neighborhood. I simply explained that I was a 1099 Traffic Monitor with company XYZ performing counts on daily vehicle traffic. Depending on the count, the state would then approve grants for traffic signals, etc.

I mean... it sounded great to me, especially with the identification card and everything. Anyhow, the man left for about an hour, then returns, only to park directly behind me. This time he wasn't so nice and demanded me to leave. I didn't respond and began to exit the area. Little did I know, this would end up being a three-to-five mile chase out of the county, zig-zagging back roads, etc. I did successfully evade any further confrontation and escaped as quickly as possible. This type of incident is quite rare and has only happened to me twice. Approximately 99% of companies that hire investigators to conduct surveillance require that you break surveillance upon being burned, a.k.a. caught in action. This, of course, can become a liability to them if anything horrible happened.

Just remember it's good to trust, but always verify.

SPEAR PHISHING

Similar to phishing, which is sending communications to individuals or employees in attempt to receive sensitive information. Phishing is typically conducted through email, and the sensitive information they're asking for is typically login credentials. Phishing emails come for people pretexting as a person associated with a specific company that a victim works for or uses. In many cases, the victim receives a scam email from a domain that is one letter or number off from the original domain used by the legitimate company. Spear Phishing is the same exact concept, however, the victim is a very specific target. Hence the word "spear".

VISHING

Vishing is simply phishing, but with only voice. Therefore, if a victim receives a phone call from someone pretending to be from a company they use or work for to gain sensitive information, this is vishing. A common type of vishing is when attackers call elder individuals and pretend to be from Medicare or the Social Security office for their state. These attackers are looking for the victim's date of birth and social security number in attempt to use for fraudulent purposes. Moving forward, if anyone calls you unexpectedly, never give any personally identifiable information over the phone. Inform them that you will hang up and call the company or office directly, then give over your sensitive information. Unfortunately, 100% of the time, these potential attacks are completed using burner numbers, therefore, a simple trace of the number will never suffice. These days, instead of buying an actual burner number, one can simply download free or paid apps that give any phone an additional burner number. As many as a person wants. The hardened criminal still prefers a physical burner phone to ditch in the event that an agency begins tracing back cell signals.

HONEY TRAP

Honey Traps are social engineering attacks that are performed by males or females that pose that they're romantically interested in a target in attempt to extract sensitive data. Though this type of social engineering is less common, it's primarily seen in government agencies, large corporations, and even divorce and custody cases. Though honey traps aren't illegal when used for divorce and custody cases, they're definitely viewed as unethical, and more than likely, any information obtained during these interactions will be thrown out of court.

A pretty famous and recent example of a honey trap is when U.S. Congressman, Eric Swalwell, had a three-year romantic relationship with a spy for the Chinese government, Fang Fang (aka Christine Fang). Though the details of what type of information was relayed from Swalwell, he was in a position of access to much, much classified information.

He held positions with:

- Permanent Select Committee on Intelligence
- Subcommittee on Intelligence Modernization & Readiness
- Subcommittee on Strategic Technologies & Advanced Research
- Committee on the Judiciary
- Subcommittee on Courts, the Internet, & Intellectual Property
- Subcommittee on Regulatory Reform, Commercial & Antitrust Law
- Committee on Homeland Security

In modern days, we see more and more types of online honey traps. I'm sure everyone has heard of the term, "catfish". People will use the photos of attractive males and females to initiate conversations with multiple people. On many occasions, you see this type of social engineering end with the individual asking a person for money for some random reason. After weeks or months of speaking to a false person online, sometimes feelings can be created from the victim to the scammer. This allows the social engineer to ask for funds with ease. Primary targets for this type of fraud are senior citizens and older adults that are less familiar with social media and the most recent online scams. It's unfortunate, but it's our current reality.

SMS PHISHING

SMS Phishing is simply a phishing tactic that is conducted via text messages. There are a variety of ways social engineering attacks can happen only through text, especially when used along with another type like vishing or phishing emails. For instance, if you ever receive an email or social media message asking for you to provide a person with the recent pin code that was just sent to your phone, an attacker is currently attempting to reset a password on one of your accounts. Never relay your pin code to anyone unless you requested it and are typing it yourself.

Again, never give out sensitive information to anyone that randomly contacts you. Always call or email back when you can verify the legitimacy of their site, email, or number.

PHYSICAL ENTRIES

Though social engineering has become more popular with the influx of technological strategies, in-person social engineering attacks are still very much so alive and kicking. Facilities typically have locking mechanisms, metal detectors, and front desk receptionists for a reason. There's always potential for a place of business to become a target, especially if that place of business houses specific or sensitive information that may benefit another person or business. I know our minds tend to drift toward robbery for financial gain when thinking of an attacker entering a place of business, but sometimes, information can be just as valuable. What about account numbers? Employee information? Client lists? What about physically stealing data from hard drives?

No, I am not referring to individuals entering the building with a firearm. I am referring to sly individuals entering with a clever pretext. For instance, it takes very little effort to dress up as an I.T. employee from a third party. The same is true for an electrician, furniture repairman, etc.

For example, let's say there is someone that is attempting to physically extract data from your manager's office. After a quick Google search or glance at the company website, they know the exact name of the person they're looking for. The attacker then throws some worn work-clothes on with a fake badge and business card. The contact number on the card goes directly to their burner phone number. That person waits for this manager to leave for lunch, then approaches the reception desk. This person then informs the receptionist the named manager requested a service call on an electrical outlet and that they were in the area. This person can even write up a fake ticket with all the identifying information necessary on it.

So far, everything checks out for the receptionist,

wouldn't you say? All this person needs is access to the office. Once they're in, they're alone with the computer, as well as other physical documents, etc. There are a million scenarios, in which, this would work. Without any solid security protocols, the attacker wins every time.

What if there were an easier way to enter a place of business without having to go through the front entrance or speak to anyone? Well, there is.

Other types of physical entries include tailgating with other employees or using a door that had been propped open for employees that smoke throughout the day. Have you ever witnessed a vehicle follow another vehicle through an open gate of a gate-guarded neighborhood. This is a simple and easy concept. Though the amount of individuals attempting to enter buildings are significantly less in numbers, it only takes one successful attempt to do a lot of damage. Again, simple security protocols can prevent this type of attack.

In conclusion, these are only the primary methods of

social engineering attacks. There are many more, and they're always evolving, unfortunately. Knowing the basic concepts of each type of attack will reduce the potential of becoming a victim. In addition, being informed on the basic types of social engineering attacks will help you recognize evolved and more complex methods moving forward.

GENERAL SECURITY MEASURES

Now let's go over some general security measures, especially for the workplace. Yes, as I have mentioned, there is no way to be 100% guarded in this day of technology. However, the more safeguards you can utilize and enforce, the harder of a target that you or your workplace become. Though I am primarily covering the use within the scope of employment, these practices will absolutely help deter potential attackers from your home and self as well.

VPN

A VPN is a Virtual Private Network that can be used

24/7, whether it's on a phone or computer. This provides security to each of your internet transmissions, even when a hacker has potentially hacked the network you're using. In other words, if you are A attempting to go to Z, this will prevent B, C, or D from interfering with that transmission. VPNs are even used in countries where access to specific sites are blocked. By using a VPN, it can act as if the signal is coming from another country, therefore, allowing a blocked site to become accessible.

There are many brands of VPNs to use. My personal favorite has always been IPVanish due to their company not keeping track or storing the sites you have visited using the VPN. You can also download a version for your phone and computer as well. By the time this is written, that information is still true and it costs approximately $15 a month.

In conclusion, VPNs are very useful, cheap, and much-needed for this era of digital fraud and hacking.

LOCKED ENTRANCES

Locked entrances are a given, are they not? However, people tend to lean on the side of convenience instead of security. Understandable, but how many times does it take for a catastrophe to happened with an unlocked door? Only once.

Something you'll see, especially with law firms, is that their front door is always locked and requires being buzzed in to enter. Dealing with unhappy legal clients can definitely hold a risk more than others, but all places of business always risk that one crazy person that woke up on the wrong side of the bed. I'm definitely not suggesting that you should treat your place of work like Fort Knox, but simple barriers like card-accessed doors can really go a long way in terms of security.

USB DROPS

If you've ever attended any type of onboarding classes, then you've been told to never stick an unknown USB drive into your computer, but do they ever explain why? Well, there are two primary reasons you should never use unknown USB drives.

The main reason is that attackers like to conduct USB drops with pre-loaded malware. This malware can quickly infect the entire computer and/or network in just a matter of seconds. In some cases, it will require a ransom of money to be transferred prior to its removal. In other cases, it may simply just steal all of the available data, all because of a simple plug into the computer.

The secondary reason is something called a USB Killer. This is when attackers leave behind a USB drive that has the capability to unleash high voltage to your system once it's plugged in. After this instant nightmare, you may as well say goodbye to your computer because it's gone forever. USB Killers are a bit more rare than malware-loaded USB drives, however, they still exist, and still serve a purpose to some strategy-driven individuals out there.

In conclusion, never be too sure when plugging anything into your phone or computer. Always know the source. Always verify. Again, it only takes one mess up to create a huge catastrophe. Continue to be a hard target.

REQUEST/VERIFY IDENTIFICATION

Requesting and verifying identification cards from strangers is vital to prevent social engineering attacks. Hopefully, if you've read the book this far, then you understand the potential versatility of individuals that practice to be sly. There are a million scenarios that can be cooked up by one half-brilliant person. Let's take the scenario from earlier where the manager of a company had the so-called electrical outlet issue. In that scenario, the reception desk was never informed by the manager of a technician coming, yet was still fooled. Well, let's say the manager informs the receptionist that a technician will be there around lunchtime, but the social engineer is also aware of this information and shows up prior to the actual technician? That means, the receptionist was waiting for a specific type of person, a person matching that description shows up with the proper attire and a business card. Why should the receptionist be weary if everything seems to check out? A simple identification card verification would more-than-likely halt the possible hack. Yes, that is a pretty rare scenario, however, it's better to be overly prepared than under. Never underestimate the mind of the common social engineer. If they're in dire need of specific information, they will live to outsmart you at every turn.

PERIPHERAL VISION

If you're unfamiliar with the term, peripheral vision, it's the total vision from all the areas around what you're directly looking at. This is the farthest vision to the left, right, up, and down. You can see things with your peripheral vision, but also not really. You can't explain in detail what you're seeing in fine details as if you were staring directly at it. However, you still observe that something exists. This is the most important part. Peripheral vision allows us to be aware of our surroundings without having to pay sole attention to it.

I once attended a school for three weeks and we were ONLY allowed to use our peripheral vision while we were there. The first day or two was a bit weird, of course. It's unnatural. However, creating a new pattern to live by, and quickly I may add, completely shaped us for the best of the rest of our lives. The school was very beneficial because it forced us to only use our peripheral vision. If I were to tell someone today to only use their peripheral vision for a week, they may succeed in doing it for only thirty minutes. People quickly get lazy and complacent. This is why building new patterns in your mind is an art-form.

After three weeks of using only this type of vision, I noticed that not only was I very proficient in military-styled operations, but just generally in life. After almost twenty years since I've taken the course, I still use my peripheral vision, religiously. Awareness is a vague term, of course. When you practice a new pattern like this, it applies to many different aspects of your life. For instance, my driving skills increased. I can see everything that's happening 15 seconds into the future.

This is exactly how you should treat the security of your life, workplace, and everything. Be aware and ahead of time. Always know the next move. Always be observing and analyzing your surroundings.

The more you practice this, the less you will even realize you're doing it. It becomes muscle memory.

SOCIAL ENGINEERING IN THE MEDIA

HISTORICAL

BARBARA CORCORAN

(2020) Barbara Corcoran from Shark Tank lost $388,000 in one email phishing scam. She received an email from what appeared to be her assistant. The email address was nearly identical to her assistant's, with only one letter out of place. The hackers knew she used a German renovation company for one of her real estate projects and they simply requested a payment via the fake assistant's email address.

Without hesitation, Barbara paid the amount in full.

As you can tell in this example, the more clients, employees, and vendors you have, the easier it is for finer details to escape you. Although anyone could have made this mistake, it's imperative to verify the small details of communications like this, especially when dealing with any type of financial transaction.

TOYOTA

(2019) A European subsidiary of Toyota was attacked by a Business Email Compromise (BEC), resulting in the loss of $37 million dollars. Toyota's finance and accounting department was contacted via email by, which appeared to be, a known business partner of their company. After very little work, the hacker was able to convince employees to deposit $37 million dollars to their foreign bank accounts.

Again, and I will say this a million times, but make sure you're always verifying what you think you know. This example was essentially Social Engineering 101. If a person or entity takes an authoritative stance and appear to check out, more than half of the times they attempt to defraud, they will succeed.

ETHEREUM

(2017) Ethereum, an upcoming cryptocurrency, had their site hacked, causing many users to lose thousands of dollars. In this attack, the hacker contacted the site's domain registry while disguising himself as the owner. After obtaining access to the site, the hacker directed the site to run from his server and siphoned funds from many users.

In this example, we see a type of company that should have far more experience with social engineering and potential hacks, yet still managed to be taken advantage of in one of the easiest ways possible. No one is immune to social engineering attacks, therefore, it's important to refresh your skills and keep up-to-date with new methods of attacks.

Complacency, especially in the workplace, can become your biggest downfall when it comes to preventative measures against hackers. Never get too comfortable with the standard way of operating. Always look for ways to improve your awareness for yourself, and of course, your place of work as well.

MOVIES WITH SOCIAL ENGINEERING

There are many movies out there floating around on the topic of social engineering, however, I will give you my top two. The two movies listed below are perfect examples of this type of work, and can broaden your mind when it comes to creating awareness on the subject.

Attn: There may be some spoilers.

MATCHSTICK MEN

In Matchstick Men (2003), Nicholas Cage uses social engineering tactics to defraud people and businesses as a full-time career. During the movie, he teaches different techniques to his newly found daughter. However, near the end, we find out that the daughter had manipulated him the entire time. This is just another case of when the master becomes the student.

This movie is a must for people who have not seen it. Though my decision may be a bit biased because I've always been a big Cage fan. As a matter of fact, Face Off is a fairly decent example of social engineering as well.

CATCH ME IF YOU CAN

In Catch Me if You Can (2002), Leonard DiCaprio plays as a professional social engineer from a young age. Throughout the film, DiCaprio uses many different disguises such as an Attorney, Doctor, and Pilot to defraud the public. This movie was based on a true story about Frank Abagnale. Due to Frank's specialties, he was recruited by the Federal Bureau of Investigation where he still administers training to this day.

HOW DO YOU PREVENT SOCIAL ENGINEERING?

INCREASED AWARENESS

Just like anything, the more you practice, the better you will become. Your primary goal for social engineering awareness and communication intelligence is to practice it to the point that it becomes second nature. Eventually, and sometimes not-so-long at all, you will begin to act and think differently without even thinking about it. This is because you created new patterns in your mind by practicing them over and over.

OPEN-SOURCE INTELLIGENCE

The best way to become more aware about open-source intelligence in regard to yourself is simply to do research. You may take some notes from this book to conduct full research on yourself or even hire a private investigator to conduct a full background check. It's smart to know what is out there floating around and how to remove as much as possible. Some sites will allow you to pay them for removal, but in my experience, it's definitely not worth it. These types of sites that house public information are a dime a dozen. For each one you remove, two more will pop up. However, this is not a lost cause. From this day on, start using your public information more wisely. That includes information that may become public at some point as well.

HUMAN INTELLIGENCE

Human Intelligence is one of the easiest subjects to master. It simply requires to you to practice people-watching. I can't speak for everyone, but a lot of people consider this a hobby. Nevertheless, the practice of watching the public allows you to master your human observation skills. You can compare and contrast how many people are the same, how many are different, how many are in a rush, how many are consumed by their phone, etc. There are a million characteristics you can pick up on by just sitting back and watching. The more you do this, the better you'll get at it. Of course, this is just like anything. For example, if you see someone wearing gym shorts, shoes, and shirt, you'll inevitably conclude that they're engaging in physical fitness either before or after you see them. The thought process of sliding these tiny clues together may take a minute or two. If you spend a lot of time people-watching or generally observing traits of the public, your mind will add these clues together in mere seconds. Similar to doing basic math. If I tell you to add six and five together, you can see it in your mind and immediately know the answer. However, when you were first asked this in elementary school, you more-than-likely counted numbers on your fingers. The more you practice, the easier work becomes. In addition, I must say that practicing Human Intelligence is one of the easiest things you can do, therefore, there's no reason to not be an expert.

INCREASED SECURITY PROTOCOLS

If you see an unsafe area or potential opening for an outsider's attack, notify your management. There's no such thing as being too safe.

Do you own security cameras at your home? Where do they point, exactly? What I've noticed while obtaining hundreds of surveillance captures is that individuals typically have their cameras pointed toward the home or business. Having cameras pointed outward are just as important if not more. If they're in a vehicle, you could have captured their license plate information. This would be pretty helpful for law enforcement, that's for sure. If they were on foot, which way did they go? East? West? South? North? More than the positioning of just security cameras, it's important that your mind starts to think this way. It's always the naive and oblivious people that get taken advantage of and this is because social engineers, hackers, and burglars know their targets pretty well.

Again, and I will continue to reiterate these things, complacency and lack of verification will inevitably be your downfall. If you leave an unlocked door, it's only a matter of time before a stranger walks in.

HIRING PENETRATION TESTERS

If you're interested in testing the susceptibility of a hack for a company, you should consider hiring a third-party Penetration Tester. Penetration testers are hired by higher management to conduct hack attempts. This includes phishing emails and in-person social engineering methods to extract a specific type of information. Hiring a penetration tester can easily bring any security vulnerabilities to light.

BE THE ENGINEER

In the event that you come across someone that is

potentially attempting to use social engineering attacks on you, one of the best ways to combat this is to act as the social engineer, yourself. This doesn't just apply to individuals you assume have the potential to take advantage of you, this can equally apply to all types of people across the board. Remember, the goal of the social engineer is to extract information from a person or entity. You can easily do the same.

Use the basics. Create rapport just as a social engineer would do. Be friendly, be nice, be an open door to the best of their knowledge. Ask questions. There is so much power in asking questions. Have you ever seen a scummy politician get cornered on live news with a question they don't want to answer? What do they do? They redirect the conversation by following up with another question. They answer a question with a question. Especially in the realm of social engineering, eventually a hacker will run out of pre-loaded answers. If you keep asking questions, getting more specific each time, eventually they'll find a breaking point or break their so-called task.

With that being said, if you are asked a question that you are uncomfortable with answering, just deflect with humor. What I mean by that is sometimes a question will be asked and your initial and defensive response of "no" may ruin the conversational vibe. To keep this up, simply play dumb as mentioned earlier and use humor. Make light of the situation or whatever they say. Joke about it. Deflect and make the other person reset and try again. As simple and stupid as that sounds, you just put up a locked gate that the other person, now, has to figure out how to enter. Easy day. Besides, we all like to laugh. Everyone wins.

RED FLAGS

What are red flags? This is nearly an irrelevant paragraph because everyone reading this book knows what a red flag is. As a matter of fact, they're smart enough to know and understand the things I'm about to list off. The purpose of reading this and me listing this off is to reiterate the specifics. Unfortunately, we are humans. We need to see things a few times before we know them, and see them a million times before it's muscle memory. Therefore, here are a few.

UNKNOWN EMAIL ACCOUNTS

As explained before, be weary of accounts of emails you do not recognize. It's to easy to disguise emails and use social engineering attacks to hack a person or company. Of course, if you're the first sender of an email and receive a response, there's no reason to act in the paranoia. I'm specifically speaking about random emails, or emails that don't make much sense. Always investigate them further. First, start with the address of the email, secondly, especially if you're not confident, ask follow up questions to the sender to VERIFY their credentials.

EXTRA CURIOUS INDIVIDUALS

We spoke about "playing dumb" earlier in this book, however, there's a thin line between playing dumb, being dumb, and just being overly curious. 100% of the time you should always raise your ears and open your eyes to anyone that is being overly curious about yourself, your business, or business operations. Typically, these people are prying for information. Rely on the information in this book. Start asking questions. The questions can be simple or complex. Start with simple questions so the potential hacker doesn't know that you're aware of their tactics. Ask questions and if the social engineer runs into a wall, they'll either leave or make a drastic movement. Both will be noticeable.

With this being said, it's imperative to reiterate to yourself and others about the type of people who contact you. Yes, stereotyping works. If anyone says otherwise, they are wrong. Is this a legitimate business? Do they have have a legitimate identification card?

Most importantly, do they have sense of urgency? A sense of urgency typically implies a person needs to complete an act within a specific amount of time. Individuals with appointments do not have this.

THE MOST IMPORTANT ELEMENT

Do not stick out. That's it. It seems simple, yet so many people mess this part up. Keep quiet, shut up.

As soon as you add your name and face to a public comment, or sign up to a new program, you are now a new target. Stash this into your thought-process, moving forward.

www.ingramcontent.com/pod-product-compliance
Lightning Source LLC
Chambersburg PA
CBHW031424210526
45464CB00005B/2037